Helping Children See Jesus

ISBN: 978-1-64104-030-3

The Lord–He Is God
Old Testament Volume 25:
Kings, Chronicles, Minor Prophets Part 3

Authors: Katherine E. Hershey (Kings/Chronicles);
Gertrude Landis (Minor Prophets)
Illustrator: Vernon Henkel
Computer Graphic Artists: Olivia and Bethany Moy
Page Layout: Patricia Pope

© 2022 Bible Visuals International
PO Box 153, Akron, PA 17501-0153
Phone: (717) 859-1131
www.biblevisuals.org

All rights reserved. No part of this publication may be reproduced, stored in a retrieval system or transmitted in any form by any means, electronic, mechanical, photocopy, recording or otherwise, without the prior permission of the publisher, except as provided by USA copyright law.

RELATED ITEMS

To access related items (such as activities, memory verse posters and translated texts) please visit our web store at www.biblevisuals.org and enter 2025 at the top right of the web page. You may need to reduce the zoom setting to get the search box.

FREE TEXT DOWNLOAD

To obtain a FREE printable copy of the English teaching text (PDF format) under Product Format, please scroll down and select Extra–PDF Teacher Text Download. Then under Language select English before clicking the ADD TO CART button to place in your shopping cart. Other languages are available at an additional cost from the Language menu. When checking out, use coupon code XTACSV17 at checkout and click on Apply Coupon to receive the discount on the English text.

- 15 -

Turn unto the LORD your God: for He is gracious and merciful, slow to anger, and of great kindness. Joel 2:13b

Lesson 1
GOD DOES NOT CHANGE

NOTE TO THE TEACHER

The four lessons is this volume emphasize tremendous characteristics of the Lord God. He, the Creator of the universe, is high above all. We, His people, should worship Him. Let your reverence of God be an example to your students.

Included in this series on Kings and Chronicles, are some prophecies of five Minor Prophets. Mr. Ivan Allbutt (a member of our Editorial Board) writes: "The last 12 books of the Old Testament are sometimes called the Minor Prophets. They are equally as important, and as surely inspired by God, as are the other prophetic books. They all tell of the judgments of God on (1) Israel and Judah, (2) their neighbors and (3) the whole earth. They all show God's mercy in the midst of judgment. And they all, in some degree, point to the return of the Lord Jesus Christ to this earth. They speak also of the establishing of His kingdom with Jerusalem as the world capital. And they tell of a wonderful new world order yet to come. Each prophet has his own special message form God. Together they show us glimpses of mercy shining through judgments."

We urge you to study carefully the prophetic books. In *The Prophets Still Speak* by F. J. Meldau, published by Friends of Israel, the word prophet and the prophets' names are printed in bold type to help locate prophecies.

It is not necessary to use the names of all those who are involved in these lessons. Names enclosed in parentheses are for your help, Teacher. Your students will not need to know them.

The map is on the back inside cover. Be sure to show students the places named in the lessons.

Scripture to be studied: 2 Chronicles 22:11-24:25; 2 Kings 11:2-12:21; Joel 1:1-3:21

The *aim* of the lesson: To show that God never changes.

What your students should *know*: God honors those who honor Him; He disciplines those who turn from Him.

What your students should *feel*: A desire to stand true for God.

What your students should *do*: Confess and forsake all known sin.

Lesson outline (for the teacher's and students' notebooks):
1. God remembers His own (2 Chronicles 22:11-12; 2 Kings 11:2-3).
2. God honors His own (2 Chronicles 23:1-21; 2 Kings 11:4-21).
3. God uses His own (2 Chronicles 24:4-14; 2 Kings 12:4-15).
4. God disciplines His own (2 Chronicles 24:2, 17-27; Joel 1:1-3:21).

The verse to be memorized:

Turn unto the LORD your God: for He is gracious and merciful, slow to anger, and of great kindness. (Joel 2:13b)

THE LESSON
1. GOD REMEMBERS HIS OWN
2 Chronicles 22:11-12; 2 Kings 11:2-3

One-year-old Joash was hidden in the great temple in Jerusalem. Only a few people knew he was there. Joash's uncle, Jehoiada, and aunt (Jehosheba) took care of him. Uncle Jehoiada was the high priest. Because he loved and served God, he taught Joash to love God.

Show Illustration #1

Some years later, Uncle Jehoiada surprised young Joash. He said, "Joash, you are the only one left of the family of King David. Long ago God made this promise to King David: 'Your family and your kingdom will be forever.' (See 2 Samuel 7:16.) Your grandmother (Athaliah) is presently the queen. But she is not from King David's family. Because she wanted to be queen, she did something very wicked. She began murdering all her grandsons. And she believes you, too, were murdered. You, Joash, were a tiny baby and your loving aunt miraculously rescued you. You were hidden then and have since lived here in God's temple. Your wicked grandmother has probably forgotten you. But the Lord remembers you, Joash. He loves you and has allowed me to care for you. Some day, Joash, you will be king of Judah."

God did remember Joash. He also remembers us.

2. GOD HONORS HIS OWN
2 Chronicles 23:1-21; 2 Kings 11:4-21

One day the leaders of Judah gathered at God's temple. The high priest, Jehoiada, announced, "Seven (7)-year-old Joash is the real king of Judah. Joash is of David's family. And God will keep His promise to David. Joash will reign as king!"

The leaders were amazed. One of David's family was alive! They were seeing him with their very own eyes. Now was the time for young Joash to be king!

Jehoiada gave the leaders orders. "On the Sabbath day, separate into three (3) groups. One group will guard the palace. Another group will guard the temple. The third group will guard the gate near the temple. The men on duty in the temple will guard King Joash. If anyone enters the temple, put him to death. Stay close to the king wherever he goes."

On the Sabbath day, the leaders swarmed in and around the temple. All stood at attention, holding spears and shields.

Then Jehoiada brought out young Joash and crowned him king. "Here, Joash, is a copy of God's Law," Jehoiada said. He and his sons poured oil on Joash's head. Then Jehoiada announced, "Joash, you are king of Judah!" The crowd clapped their hands and shouted, "LONG LIVE THE KING!"

Show Illustration #2

Wicked Queen Athaliah, hearing the noise, ran to the temple. She saw young King Joash standing at the temple entrance. With him were the officers and the trumpeters. The people were singing happily while men played musical instruments. Everyone was thrilled to have a new king. Old Athaliah tore her robes and screamed, "Treason! Treason!"

["You have turned against me. You have rebelled against me! You are not loyal to me!"]

Jehoiada commanded, "Get her out of here! If anyone takes her part, kill him! Get rid of her!"

Wicked Athaliah was rushed out of the temple and put to death. (This was punishment for her wickedness and idolatry.)

Jehoiada told the people, "You belong to the Lord. Be loyal to him!"

The crowd promised to be true to the Lord. Immediately they went to the idol temple and destroyed it. Afterward, King Joash was taken to the palace. There they seated him on the king's big throne. God honored young Joash.

A seven-year-old could not make the important decisions of a king. So Uncle Jehoiada and others helped to rule Judah, the Southern Kingdom. Later, when Joash grew older, he would rule by himself.

3. GOD USES HIS OWN
2 Chronicles 24:4-14; 2 Kings 12:4-15

King Joash decided God's temple must be repaired. Nearly 150 years had passed since the magnificent temple was built. Certain kings who reigned during those years, did not love the Lord. So the temple had not been cared for.

King Joash called the priests together. "Go to the towns of Judah!" he commanded. "Collect the money which the people owe to God. This money will be used to repair the temple."

When the priests were slow to obey King Joash, he announced a new plan: "We shall set a chest by the altar in the temple. The people can place their gifts in the chest when they come to worship."

At the command of the king, Jehoiada made a chest. He bored a hole in the lid of it. He set it on the right side of the altar. Then King Joash sent an announcement to all the people. "Bring your money gifts to the temple when you come to worship."

Show Illustration #3

Immediately the people gladly obeyed. They brought their money and dropped it into the chest. They gave so much that the chest had to be emptied many times. How happy the people were! We, too, are happy when we give to the work of the Lord.

Soon there was enough money. The carpenters, masons, stonecutters and others went to work. The temple was repaired and the workmen were paid. Again the temple was used to worship God. The Bible says, "The people offered burnt offerings in the house of the Lord continually all the days of Jehoiada" (2 Chronicles 24:14). God used His own people to do His work. And the Lord still uses His people in His work.

Jehoiada, the High Priest, lived to be an old man. (He was 130 when he died.) After his death, something very sad happened.

4. GOD DISCIPLINES HIS OWN
2 Chronicles 24:2, 17-27; Joel 1:1-3:21

Some of the wicked leaders of Judah talked to King Joash. Wicked men usually speak wickedly. The king listened to them and, amazingly, he turned away from God. Instead of being strong for the Lord, King Joash turned away from Him. King Joash stopped worshiping at God's temple which he himself had repaired. Rather than leading his men to God, Joash followed them to their idols. King Joash sinned, and God hates sin.

The Lord God was angry with the king and people of Judah. But He still loved them. So He sent **prophets** to try to bring them back to Him. (See 2 Chronicles 24:19.) One **prophet**, JOEL, said the words of our verse: ". . . Turn to the Lord your God. He is gracious and merciful, slow to anger, and of great kindness" (Joel 2:13). (Have students repeat the verse.)

The **prophet JOEL** gave this warning: "Hear this, you elders! Listen, all who live in the land. Has anything like this ever happened in your days or the days of your fathers?" (See Joel 1:1-2.) Then he told of a dreadful army-like swarm of locusts. They ate everything in the fields. The grain, grapes, all the trees were destroyed by the locusts. Even the animals suffered. Nothing, not even water, was left. (See 1:4, 11-12.) Why did God allow such destruction? Because the people had sinned by turning from the Lord.

Show Illustration #4

JOEL told more in his prophecy. He said, "The day of the Lord–a day of great trouble (tribulation)–is coming!" (See Joel 2:1.) The prophet JOEL spoke these words long, long ago (about 800 years before Christ came to earth). But "the day of the Lord" has not come, even yet. "That day," JOEL said, "will be a day of darkness and gloom. It will be a day of clouds and blackness. A large and mighty army will come (an army much more fierce than locusts). Before this army comes, the land will be as beautiful as the garden of Eden. After the army goes, nothing will be left. All will be destroyed by blazing fire." (See 2:2-3.) JOEL continued his warning, saying, "The day of the Lord is dreadful. Who can endure it? Listen to the words of the Lord: 'Return to Me with all your heart'." (See 2:11-12.) God is always calling His people to return to Him. He longs to forgive His own.

Do you belong to the family of God? If so, you will not be here on earth during the awful day of the Lord. You will be safe in heaven.

JOEL closed his prophecy with good news to follow the day of the Lord. God said, "Judah and Jerusalem shall be lived in forever. I shall pardon them." (See 3:20-21.)

King Joash and his men heard the warnings of the **prophets**. But they refused to return to God. Finally the Lord sent Zechariah, Uncle Jehoiada's son. Zechariah stood before the people and announced: "This is what God says: 'Why do you disobey the Lord's commands? You will not prosper. Because you have turned away from the Lord, He has turned away from you'." (See 2 Chronicles 24:20.)

The king and his wicked friends didn't like what Zechariah said. King Joash commanded, "Stone him to death!" And it was done.

Think of it! King Joash was alive because Zechariah's father, Jehoiada, had cared for him. Joash no longer cared about his Uncle Jehoiada's kindness. So he killed Jehoiada's son, Zechariah. As long as his uncle, Jehoiada, had lived, Joash followed the Lord. (See 2 Chronicles 24:2.) But evil men had turned him away from God.

It is easy to please God when you are with other Christians. But how do you live when you are with godless people? Suppose they make fun of Christians or laugh at the Bible.

What do you say? What do you do when they swear or lie or cheat? Do you turn away from God as Joash did?

For his sin, the Lord disciplined King Joash. He caused a small group from the Syrian Army to march into Jerusalem. (Jerusalem was Judah's capital city. Show Jerusalem and Syria on the map.) There the Syrians battled Judah's large army. The Syrians killed the leaders who had turned Joash away from God. (See 2 Chronicles 24:23-24.) God gave the Syrians victory over His very own people. Why? Because King Joash and Judah had turned away from God.

King Joash wanted the Syrians to get out of Jerusalem. So he grabbed the sacred gold treasures from God's temple and the palace. To the Syrians, Joash commanded, "Take these to your king!" The Syrian army snatched the golden valuables and hurried home. God's wonderful treasures went to the enemy! (See 2 Kings 12:18.)

Joash's servants, angry because Joash had killed Jehoiada's son, murdered Joash. Joash's son (Amaziah) then became the new king of Judah. So someone from David's family was still on the throne, exactly as God had promised.

Because King Joash turned away from God, God disciplined him. The Lord does not change. He still disciplines those who turn from Him. (*Teacher:* God does not always use death as His discipline. But see 1 Corinthians 11:27-31; 1 John 5:16.)

Have you turned from God? Are you doing anything which displeases Him? (*Teacher:* You may want to read Ephesians 4:30-32.) The Bible says, "It is a fearful thing to fall into the hands of the living god" (Hebrews 10:31). Do not make it necessary for the Lord to discipline you. He loves you and wants to forgive any wrong you have done. Will you this moment confess your sin to Him? (See Proverbs 28:13; 1 John 1:9.)

Teacher: Allow a time of quiet for the Lord to speak to each one.

Lesson 2
GOD ALWAYS DOES RIGHT

NOTE TO THE TEACHER

History is the record of what has happened. Prophecy tells us what will happen. The Bible books of Kings and Chronicles contain important history. God's people could have had God Himself as their King. Instead, they chose to have earthly kings like their neighboring nations. These four books tell the problems caused by some of the earthly kings. Certain kings began well. Most failed God and His people.

God loved His people and did not want to have to punish them. So He sent prophets who warned what would happen if they disobeyed Him. When God's people refused to turn back to Him, He had to punish them. So the prophecies came true. However, most prophets also prophesied certain events which have not yet even occurred. Because God's Word is true, everything the propehts said will come true. The Lord God has a planned order of events. All will take place in His time.

The chronicles [detailed historical record of events] of these Old Testament kings should be examples to your students. May the Lord use the prophets' fore-tellings to warn and comfort us all.

Included in this lesson are these words: plundered, spoil, loot, plunder, booty. All refer to stealing by force. Explain and use the one word your students will easily remember.

Scripture to be studied: 2 Chronicles 25:1-26:23; 2 Kings 14:1-21; 15:1-7, 32; Amos 1:1-9:15

The *aim* of the lesson: To show that God does right in punishing the proud.

What your students should *know*: We have no reason to be proud because all we are or have comes from God.

What your students should *feel*: A sense of humility, since God's goodness is not deserved.

What your students should *do*: Confess all pride to the Lord. Forsake idol-worship. Thank God for His loving promises.

Lesson outline (for the teacher's and students' notebooks):
1. God leads His own (2 Chronicles 25:1-13; 2 Kings 14:1-2).
2. God hates pride in His own (2 Chronicles 25:14-28; 2 Kings 14:8-14).
3. God helps His own (2 Chronicles 26:1-15; 2 Kings 14:21).
4. God punishes His own (2 Chronicles 26:16-23; 2 Kings 15:32; Amos 1:1-9:15).

The verse to be memorized:

Turn unto the LORD your God: for He is gracious and merciful, slow to anger, and of great kindness. (Joel 2:13b)

THE LESSON

Joash, who became king of Judah as a boy, started well. As a man, he did a great work. Who will tell what he did? (Let students discuss Joash's getting funds for and repairing God's temple. With questions, continue reviewing Joash's life.) Finally King Joash refused to listen to God's prophets. He would not return to God. So the Lord allowed him to be murdered. Joash, of King David's family, lost the throne and his life. His 25-year-old son, Amaziah, became Judah's next king. Together let us read 2 Chronicles 25:2: Amaziah did what "was right in the sight of the Lord, but not with a perfect heart." Does this sound good? bad? both? Listen carefully!

1. GOD LEADS HIS OWN
2 Chronicles 25:1-13; 2 Kings 14:1-2

The time came when King Amaziah decided he needed a good army. He called together all the people of Judah (the Southern Kingdom). From them he chose men who were at least 20 years old.

The men stood at attention while King Amaziah counted them. He began: "One . . . two . . . 10 . . . 20 . . . 50 . . . 100 . . . 1,000 . . . 5,000 . . . 100,000 . . . 300,000!" What an army! All 300,000 men were able to handle the spear and shield. Great soldiers!

King Amaziah planned to send his army against the land of Edom. (*Teacher:* Show Edom, inside back cover.) To be certain of a great victory, Amaziah wanted more soldiers. So he sent to Israel (the Northern Kingdom) for 100,000 men. For these, Amaziah paid lots of money. What an army he now had!

Right then a man of God (a **prophet**) came to him. "O King Amaziah!" he began. "Do not let the soldiers of Israel fight with your Judean soldiers. The Lord is not with Israel." (Remember! Israel had only bad kings who led the Israelites away from God.) The man of God said more. "If you take the soldiers of Israel with you, God will overthrow you. God has the power to help or to overthrow." The Lord was leading King Amaziah through His **prophet**.

Amaziah had a question for the **prophet**. "What about all the money I paid for these Israelite soldiers?"

The man of God had good news: "The Lord is able to give you much more than that."

Show Illustration #5

King Amaziah listened to the **prophet** and obeyed his words. He sent the Israelite soldiers to their homeland. These soldiers must have looked forward to stealing many treasures from the Edomite homes. So they were furious with Judah. They would not forget this!

King Amaziah then led his army of 300,000 to Edom. (Show on map.) There God gave him a great victory. Even with a smaller army than Amaziah had wanted, he defeated the Edomites. The Lord had led the king through the **prophet** who gave God's message.

2. GOD HATES PRIDE IN HIS OWN
2 Chronicles 25:14-28; 2 Kings 14:8-14

King Amaziah and his soldiers celebrated their victory. They had plundered the Edomites' homes, bringing back much spoil.

The king also brought home the idols of the Edomites. He set them up, burned sacrifices to them, even worshiped them! Think of it. King Amaziah worshiped idols made by men's hands! These images had eyes, but could not see. They had ears which could not hear. They had mouths which could not speak. (See Psalm 135:15-17.) King Amaziah did not thank the living God for His victory. Instead, he worshiped idols.

The Lord was angry about this. He sent a **prophet** to King Amaziah with His message: "Why do you worship the gods of the Edomites? Their gods did not save the Edomites from your army." (See 2 Chronicles 25:15.)

King Amaziah was wild with rage when he heard the **prophet's** message. He shouted, "When did we ask you to give advice to me, the King? Be quiet, or I shall have you killed!"

Quietly the **prophet** prophesied: "Because you have not listened to God's message, He will destroy you." (See 2 Chronicles 25:16.)

Now Judah's King Amaziah was in trouble–more trouble than he knew. The soldiers of Israel who had been sent home were angry. So they had attacked some cities in Judah, killing 3,000 people. (See 2 Chronicles 25:13.) They plundered houses and took home the booty. For this, King Amaziah challenged the king of Israel (Jehoash) to fight against Judah.

The king of Israel answered, "Because you defeated Edom, you are proud. Stay at home, or you and all Judah will get into trouble." (See 2 Chronicles 25:19.)

Amaziah, proud king of Judah, would not listen to the king of Israel. So the battle began. Because King Amaziah had turned to idols, God refused to help him. For this, Judah's army was defeated and King Amaziah was captured. (See 2 Chronicles 25:23.)

Show Illustration #6

The army of Israel took Judah's defeated King Amaziah back to Jerusalem. There he watched the Israelites break down some of the city wall. He saw them loot God's temple and his palace. These tremendous treasures, together with prisoners of war, were taken to Samaria (capital of Israel–show on map.) We know nothing more about Amaziah except that he was destroyed. The **prophet's** prophecy had come true.

God's word says, "Pride goes before destruction and a haughty spirit before a fall" (Proverbs 16:18). This was certainly true of King Amaziah. The Lord tried to get him to listen. He sent His **prophet** to call Amaziah away from idols, back to God. The words of our verse say what God wanted him to do. (Have students quote **Joel** 2:13b.) But Amaziah would not listen.

Do you have abilities others do not have? If so, quietly thank God. He, the One who always does right, gives abilities to His own. Pride ruined Amaziah, king of Judah; and pride can ruin you. God hates pride. (See Psalm 101:5b; Proverbs 6:16-17; 21:4.)

3. GOD HELPS HIS OWN
2 Chronicles 26:1-15; 2 Kings 14:21

Amaziah's son, Uzziah, at age 16, became Judah's next king. King Uzziah worshiped the Lord. He was a fine king who brought honor to his nation. Judah again became strong. (It was greater than at any time since King Solomon.) King Uzziah was very skillful. He was a capable builder, a cattleman, and a well digger. He knew how to grow excellent crops. He carefully organized his big army and made for them weapons of war. (*Teacher:* Depending upon the ages of your students, read to them 2 Chronicles 26:9-15.)

Show Illustration #7

King Uzziah was a very able man. The Bible says of him, "As long as he sought the Lord, God made him prosper" (2 Chronicles 26:5). It also says, "God helped Uzziah." (See 2 Chronicles 26:7.) Since Uzziah had a great army, Jerusalem was protected from enemies. Because of his abilities, King Uzziah became famous in other countries. "His fame spread far and wide, for he was marvelously helped, until he was strong." (See 2 Chronicles 26:15.) Who helped King Uzziah? The Lord was his help.

God is righteous. Because He always does right, He helps His own who seek Him. If you are a child of God, He will help you. Are you willing to ask for His help?

4. GOD PUNISHES HIS OWN
2 Chronicles 26:16-23; 2 Kings 15:32; Amos 1:1-9:15

Now, listen to God's Word. "But when Uzziah was strong, his heart was lifted up" (2 Chronicles 26:16). King Uzziah became proud. And because of pride, he did something dreadfully wrong.

King Uzziah went into the holy place in the temple. He was ready to burn incense on the altar of incense. Long before, God had commanded that only the priests could do this. (See Exodus 30:7-9; Numbers 16:40.) King Uzziah was not a priest and he knew God's command.

More than 80 priests followed the king into the holy place. Courageously they said, "It is not right for you, O King, to burn incense to the Lord. God has set apart the priests to do this. Leave the holy place. The Lord will not honor you."

King Uzziah was furious. There, inside God's holy temple, he screamed at the priests.

Show Illustration #8

As the king raged, leprosy (ugly, contagious sores) broke out on his forehead. The priests, seeing the leprosy, rushed him outside. Even Uzziah wanted to get out of God's holy place. But it was too late. The Lord had already struck the king. He would have leprosy the rest of his life. He could no longer live in his palace. He had to stay in a separate house away from other people. This was God's law for those with leprosy. (See Leviticus 13:46.) From then until he died, Uzziah's son (Jotham) did the king's work.

The Bible says, "Those who walk in pride, God is able to humble." (See Daniel 4:37.) God's humbling may come as punishment to people, cities, even entire lands. Of this you can be certain: whatever God does is always right.

At about this time, God called a shepherd, **AMOS**, to be a **prophet**. (Amos 7:15.) God sent **AMOS** to Bethel in Israel (show on map) to prophesy. (See Amos 7:12-13.) Years before, King Jeroboam of Israel had set a golden calf idol in Bethel. "Worship here," Jeroboam had commanded the Israelites. So the people had turned from the living God of heaven. They worshiped a man-made idol. God could not, would not approve of idolatry. (See Exodus 20:1-5.) Idolatry is sin. Sin must be punished. But God is always right; He is fair. He would not punish His people without warning them of their sin. For this reason the Lord sent **AMOS** to Bethel.

Show Illustration #9

AMOS announced: "The Lord roars!" (See Amos 1:2.) Surprisingly **AMOS** began by telling the sins of Israel's neighbors. (*Teacher:* Using map, point to place names as you mention them.)

The prophet **AMOS** spoke sharply: "The Lord says to Damascus, 'You have been cruel to prisoners. I shall send fire. It will destroy the king's palace and your fortresses. I shall break down the Damascus gate [leaving the city unprotected]. You people of Syria will be taken captive.'" (See 1:3-5.) [They would be taken as prisoners to another land.]

AMOS continued, "The Lord says, 'Gaza (in Philistia) captured whole communities and sold them as slaves. For this I shall send fire and destroy the cities of Philistia.'" (See 1:6-8.)

The city of Tyre heard God's rebuke for their sin. This was followed by, "I shall send fire." (See 1:9-10.) God would not overlook their sins.

AMOS also fearlessly spoke God's messages to the lands of Edom, Ammon, Moab. Their sins were not alike. But God's punishment would be the same. He said, "I shall send fire." (See 1:11-2:3.) [All three lands were later overtaken by the Assyrians.]

AMOS turned to the two tribes in Judah, his homeland. "God says, 'You have rejected the Law of the Lord. You have been led astray by false gods. I shall send fire.'" (See 2:4-5.)

Were the Israelites glad to learn that their neighbors would be punished? Probably. **AMOS**, a visitor in Israel, certainly would not speak unkindly to them. or would he? God had sent **AMOS** to Israel. So he had to speak God's message.

The prophet **AMOS** began, "The Lord says this to Israel: 'You trample on the heads of the poor. You commanded the **prophets** not to prophesy. I shall crush you. On the day I punish Israel for her sins, I shall destroy the altars of Bethel'." (See 2:6-16; 3:14.) The golden calf was not hidden from God!

The Lord said much, much more to the people of Israel. Then He added, "Because I shall do this to you, prepare to meet your God, O Israel" (Amos 4:12). God pled with His people: "Seek Me and live; do not seek Bethel [the place of the idol]. Bethel will be reduced to nothing." (See 5:4-6.)

Everything God said made the priest of Bethel angry. He told **AMOS**, "Get out! Go to Judah. Do your prophesying there. Do not prophesy any more at Bethel . . . This is the temple of Israel." (See 7:12-13.) The people of Israel loved their golden calf idol. They would not turn to the Lord who loved them.

God spoke sadly to Israel through His prophet: "'Israel will certainly go into exile, away from their native land. (See 7:17.) I shall never forget anything they have done (8:7). The eyes of the Lord are on the sinful kingdom. I shall destroy it from the face of the earth–yet not totally'" (9:8). God punishes sinning kings like Uzziah. He also punishes sinful cities and lands.

The Lord added this great news about a time which will come in the future: ". . . I shall restore David's tent. I shall repair and restore it, and build it as it used to be" (9:11-12). The Lord had promised David (300 years before this) that his kingdom would be forever. Now God renewed His promise. David's kingdom [tent] would continue, even though Uzziah, descendant of David's family, had sinned. The living God of heaven never forgets! He, the One who hates and punishes sin, remembers His loving promises. He always does right.

Do you, like King Uzziah, have a problem with pride? Will you confess it to the Lord this moment? Ask His help to turn from this sin He hates. Do you love anything or anyone more than the Lord (as did the people of Israel)? If so, will you ask God's forgiveness?

Let us all thank the Lord for His wonderful prophecies. Thank Him that they will all come true–in His time.

Lesson 3
GOD HAS ALL POWER

NOTE TO THE TEACHER

God gave the people He chose for Himself specific laws. His very first commandment is: "You shall have no other gods before me." The second command says: "you shall not make for yourself an idol . . ." (See Exodus 20:1-4.) Unnumbered times the Lord repeated these commands. When His people obeyed Him, they enjoyed His blessings. When they disobeyed, He punished them. He even became angry with them (2 Chronicles 28:25). But the Lord does not stay angry forever (Psalm 103:9). He forgave those who truly returned to Him.

During the times of the kings, God's people were particularly disobedient. Because of His loving kindness, God sent many prophets to warn them. the prophets did more than simply warn people of the consequences fo the their sin. Often they spoke of events of the future Some of these prophecies have already come true. In this lesson, Micah speaks of Samaria's becoming " a heap of stones." (See Micah 1:3-7.) This prophecy came true during the reign of King Ahaz in Judah. "The King of Assyria invaded the entire land [of Israel], marched against Samaria and laid siege to it for three years" (2 Kings 17:5). Then the Assyrians seized all Israel and took the Israelites as captives to Assyria.

All that God said would happen, will happen. He has all power and will keep His Word perfectly. Teach God's Word with conviction and urgency!

Scripture to be studied: Jonah 1:1-4:11; 2 Kings 15:32-16:20; 2 Chronicles 27:1-28:8, 16-27; Isaiah 7:1-12; Micah 1:1-7:20

The *aim* of the lesson: To show that God is the all-powerful, Almighty One.

What your students should *know:* That God never forces us to obey Him.

What your students should *feel:* A desire to obey God.

What your students should *do:* Ask God to help them to obey Him.

Lesson outline (for the teacher's and students' notebooks):

1. God is always in control (Jonah 1:1-4:11).
2. God can do anything (2 Kings 16:5-6; 2 Chronicles 28:5-8, 16-19).
3. God has power to protect His own (2 Chronicles 28:8-15; Isaiah 7:1-9).
4. God is the Almighty One (2 Kings 16:7-19; 2 Chronicles 28:20-25; Isaiah 7:10-12; Micah 1:1-7:20).

The verse to be memorized:

Turn unto the LORD your God: for He is gracious and merciful, slow to anger, and of great kindness. (Joel 2:13b)

THE LESSON

Men were often glad to be **prophets** of the living God. **ELIJAH, ELISHA, OBADIAH, JOEL, AMOS** all spoke for the Lord. They prophesied His warnings of punishment if people continued sinning. Sometimes those who heard, accepted God's messages. Too many times they ignored, or even killed, God's **prophets**. (See Acts 7:52.)

Usually the **prophets** of God prophesied in Judah and Israel. God had chosen these people for Himself. But the Lord loves all people everywhere. For this reason, He had used the prophet **AMOS** to warn neighboring cities and lands. Farther away was the city of Nineveh, capital of Assyria. (Show on map.) The wicked, cruel, Assyrians were idol-worshipers. The Lord wanted them to learn of Him. He would forgive their dreadful sins if they would turn to Him.

1. GOD IS ALWAYS IN CONTROL
Jonah 1:1-4:11

One day the Lord spoke to **JONAH**: "Go to the big city of Nineveh and preach against it. Their wickedness has come up before Me" (**Jonah** 1:2). Nineveh (capital of Assyria) was far away from Jonah's hometown, Gath-hepher. (See 2 Kings 14:25. *Teacher:* Point to place names on map.) God was asking **JONAH** to be a prophet.

JONAH knew at once what he would do. Instead of obeying God and going up to Nineveh, he went down to Joppa (a city on the Mediterranean seashore). There he boarded a ship bound for Tarshish (about 2,000 miles westward). Down in the boat, **JONAH** fell asleep.

The Lord sent a wild storm. The terrified sailors expected the ship to break apart. Each began praying to his idol. The captain woke **JONAH**, shouting, "How can you sleep? Get up! Call on your idol! Maybe he will see what is happening and help us."

JONAH immediately understood that God was punishing him for his disobedience. He knew the sailors had to get rid of him. Otherwise everyone on board ship would die.

Show Illustration #10

JONAH commanded, "Throw me overboard!" The sailors obeyed and **JONAH** went down into the sea. There the Lord had a huge fish which swallowed **JONAH**. For three days and three nights, **JONAH** was inside that great fish. Finally, **JONAH** prayed to God–and God heard him.

Show Front Cover

The Lord commanded the fish to spit **JONAH** onto dry land. Unlike **JONAH**, the fish obeyed God.

Again the Lord spoke to **JONAH**: "Go to Nineveh. Tell them the message I give you." This time **JONAH** obeyed. In Nineveh he prophesied God's message: "Forty more days and Nineveh will be overthrown." Throughout the big city, **JONAH** announced the same prophecy over and over again.

When the news reached the king, he took off his royal robes. Covering himself with sackcloth (rough cloth used for making sacks), he sat in the dust. By doing this, the king proved he was truly sorry for his sins. The king commanded, "Let everyone call urgently on God. Let them give up their evil ways and their violence. Maybe God will forgive us so we shall not perish."

God saw that the people were sorry for their sins. He immediately forgave them and did not destroy their city. This made **JONAH** angry. God was not going to overthrow Nineveh as he had prophesied. **JONAH** had been punished for his disobedience. He wanted the people of Nineveh to be punished for their wickedness. **JONAH** forgot that the people of Nineveh were truly sorry for their sins.

The living God of heaven has all power. He can send a wild storm. He can prepare a fish huge enough to swallow a man. He can call a disobedient **prophet** a second time. He can forgive wicked people who turn to Him. God is always in control.

2. GOD CAN DO ANYTHING
2 Kings 16:5-6; 2 Chronicles 28:5-8, 16-19

God has power over **prophets** like **JONAH**. He has power over kings like Uzziah of Judah. Uzziah was an excellent king– at first. He could do almost anything. But he learned there was something he could not do. He had gone proudly into the Holy Place of the temple. Only priests were allowed there. But Uzziah entered the Holy Place, ready to burn incense. The priests had tried to warn him, but King Uzziah wouldn't listen. There in the temple God immediately punished him with awful leprosy.

Uzziah's son, Jotham, became king and "did right in the eyes of the Lord." His father's leprosy reminded him of God's punishment for pride. Uzziah's son became powerful because he obeyed God.

After Uzziah's son died, Uzziah's grandson, Ahaz, became king of Judah. Like his father and grandfather, Ahaz was of the family of King David. But King Ahaz was not like King David. Ahaz did not do what was right in the eyes of the Lord. (See 2 Kings 16:2-4; 2 Chronicles 28:1-4.) He made idols and worshiped them. He even sacrificed his own children! King Ahaz paid no attention to the true and living God of heaven. And the people of Judah followed the example of their King. Did God know what King Ahaz was doing? (Encourage student discussion.) Could the Lord do anything about Ahaz and Judah? Of course He could. He who has all power can do anything.

God handed King Ahaz and Judah over to the kings of Syria and Israel. (See 2 Chronicles 28:5.)

Show Illustration #11

God allowed the neighboring armies of Syria and Israel (the Northern Kingdom) to fight against Judah (the Southern Kingdom). In one day 120,000 brave soldiers of Judah died. And 200,000 men, women, and children were captured and taken as prisoners. Why was Judah so severely defeated? "Because Judah had forsaken the Lord God." (See 2 Chronicles 28:6). We could have told King Ahaz the words of our verse. (Have students quote Joel 2:13.)

3. GOD HAS POWER TO PROTECT HIS OWN
2 Chronicles 28:8-15; Isaiah 7:1-9

King Ahaz and his people were afraid, shaking like trees in the wind. (See Isaiah 7:2.) So God sent a **prophet**, **ISAIAH**, to talk to King Ahaz. "Be careful," **ISAIAH** began. "Keep calm. Do not be afraid. Those kings of Israel and Syria have planned to destroy you. They say, 'We are going to tear Judah to pieces and divide it among ourselves. We shall get rid of Ahaz and put our man on the throne.'" (See Isaiah 7:3-6.)

Then ISAIAH gave some good news. "But God says this will not happen." (See Isaiah 7:7.) The Lord has all power. He can protect His own. He would not allow a king from another land to be on Judah's throne.

Show Illustration #12

The Lord had promised to keep David's throne in His hands. God would not let the kingdom be taken from David's family. Ahaz was wicked, but he was of the family of David. And God would keep His promise to David. (See 2 Samuel 7:11b-16.)

King Ahaz was glad for God's good news. But he loved idols more than God.

4. GOD IS THE ALMIGHTY ONE
2 Kings 16:7-19; 2 Chronicles 28:20-25;
Isaiah 7:10-12; Micah 1:1.-7:20

The time came when King Ahaz needed help. He could have turned from his sins to the Lord. God, the Almighty One, has all power. He would have helped Ahaz. Instead, King Ahaz turned to the king of Assyria. (**JONAH** the **prophet** had preached in Assyria's capital city, Nineveh.)

King Ahaz went to God's holy temple. From it he took God's treasures and sent them to the Assyrian king. (See 2 Kings 16:7-8.) "Come help me!" Ahaz begged the king of Assyria.

Instead of getting help, King Ahaz got trouble. (See 2 Chronicles 28:20.) In his time of trouble "King Ahaz became even more unfaithful to the Lord." (See 2 Chronicles 28:22.) Think of that!

Then King Ahaz visited Damascus, a neighboring city (show on map). There he saw a heathen altar. Ahaz wanted one like it and got a pattern of it. He sent it to the priest of God's holy temple in Jerusalem. "Make an altar like this for me," Ahaz commanded. And the priest whom God had set apart for Himself, obeyed the sinful king.

King Ahaz moved God's altar out of the temple. "From now on," Ahaz told the priest, "use this new altar." King Ahaz had other changes made at God's temple. All this he did to please the king of Assyria. (See 2 Kings 16:17-18.)

Finally Ahaz closed the Lord's temple. He made for himself altars at every corner in Jerusalem. In every town in Judah he built high places. On these the people of Judah burned sacrifices to other gods. The king had led the priest and people away from the living God. So King Ahaz made God angry! (See 2 Chronicles 28:25.)

God, the Almighty One, could have punished King Ahaz immediately. Instead, he sent another **prophet**, **MICAH**, to warn the king. **MICAH** began, "Hear, O people, all of you! Listen, O earth, and all who are in it! The Lord is going to punish Samaria, all Israel, Jerusalem, and all Judah! This is what the Lord says, 'I shall make Samaria a heap of stones. All its idols will be broken to pieces. (See **Micah** 1:3-7.) I, the Lord, shall send disaster to Jerusalem. The children you love will go from you into exile in another land.' " (See 1:12-16.)

MICAH told the people, "You are greedy. You are covetous (wanting for yourselves what belongs to others). So this is what the Lord says, 'I am planning disaster against you, My people. You will not be able to save yourselves.'" (See 2:1-3.)

The **prophet** spoke harshly to the leaders of the people. "You hated good and loved evil. Because of you, Jerusalem will become a heap of stones. The temple hill will be a mound overgrown with thickets." (See 3:1-12.) Their magnificent temple would be destroyed. Why? Because king and people had turned from their loving God. And God was really angry.

Show Illustration #13

Quickly the **prophet** added good news. "In the last days, the mountain of the Lord's temple will be established . . . The people will stream to it. Many nations will come and say, 'Come, let us go up to the mountain of the Lord, to the house of God. He will teach us His ways, so we may walk in His paths.' The word of the Lord will go out from Jerusalem. There will be no more wars. The Lord Almighty has spoken. We shall walk in the name of the Lord our God forever and ever." (See 4:1-5.) These "last days" of which God spoke have not come even yet. But everything will take place in His time. For He is the almighty God.

The Lord had more good news. **MICAH** prophesied to Bethlehem, the city in which King David had been born. He said, "You, Bethlehem, are small in Judah. But out of you will come One who will rule over Israel. He is from eternity." (See Micah 5:2.) King Ahaz could not understand this prophecy. But we can, because part of it has already come true. God was saying that His eternal Son would be born in Bethlehem. God's Son, the Lord Jesus, was always with God. **MICAH** prophesied He would come to Bethlehem.

Jesus did come 700 years later. But the people would not let Him be their Ruler. Instead, they put Him to death. Jesus did not stay dead. He rose again and went back to heaven. The time will come when the Lord Jesus will reign here on earth. Then, in God's time, the rest of **MICAH'S prophecy** will come true.

God's people began to understand how good God is, and how sinful they were. They wanted to be forgiven. They asked, "Will the Lord be pleased with sacrifices of thousands of rams? Or will He be pleased with 10,000 rivers of oil? Will He accept the firstborn sons as a sacrifice?" No! God did not want such sacrifices for their sins. He wanted obedience. He said, "Stop sinning. Do right. Love kindness. Walk humbly with God." (See **Micah** 6:1-8.)

God wanted His people in **MICAH'S** time to do right. He wants us to do right. And He Himself will help us. But He does not *force* us to do right. God did not force King Uzziah, **JONAH**, or King Ahaz to do right. But He punished them for doing wrong.

The Lord also wants His people to walk humbly. not proudly, with Him. Whatever we have, whatever we are, we owe to God, the Almighty One. Will you ask Him now to help you do right by obeying him? Remember, God has all power, for He is the Almighty One.

Lesson 4
GOD IS HOLY

NOTE TO THE TEACHER

Throughout this series, the focus has been on the Lord God. Your students may have difficulty remembering all the historical and prophetic facts. But teach with such clarity that the characteristics of God will remain with them always.

"God is holy." That is, He is *set apart* from all others. He is absolutely *perfect*. He is *righteous* and always does right. He is *pure*–without any sin. (See Exodus 15:11; Leviticus 19:2; Habakkuk 1:13; Revelation 4:8.) We, of course, can never be holy as God is. Yet God commands us to live lives of holiness (1 Peter 1:15-16). Make this the thrust of your teaching.

The outline of this lesson covers four points of Joel 2:13, our verse to be memorized. Keep the truths of this verse before your students. Encourage them to quote it often in the days ahead.

In your preparation for teaching this lesson, study the entire book of Hosea. He was a prophet with an aching heart. His wife had become unfaithful. So Hosea understood that God was broken-hearted because of Israel's unfaithfulness to Him. May your heart, teacher, be affected by the spiritual needs of your students. Teach with loving compassion.

In Hosea, Ephraim is mentioned 30 times. Ephraim was one of Israel's larger tribes and the name is used for Israel. Near the end of his prophetic ministry, Hosea pled again with the people of Israel. He said, "O Israel, return to the Lord thy God. Your sins caused you to fall . . . Return to the Lord. Say to Him, 'Forgive all our sins; receive us graciously. Assyria cannot save us. Never again will we speak of something man-made as our gods.' " (See Hosea 14:1-3.)

Hosea's pleading was ignored. But some day (yet in the future), Israel will turn to the Lord. According to Hosea, God will than say, "I shall forgive their sins and love them. My anger has turned from them." (See Hosea 14:4.) God is not yet finished with Israel!

Scripture to be studied: 2 Kings 17:1-41; Hosea 4:1-14:2

The *aim* of the lesson: To show that those who rebel against God will be punished.

What your students should *know*: That anything which replaces God in their lives, can be an idol.

What your students should *feel*: A desire to worship God only.

What your students should *do*: Turn truly to God, the Holy One, forsaking all idols.

Lesson outline (for the teacher's and students' notebooks):
1. God is gracious (Joel 2:13; Hosea 4:1-2; 11:1-8; 13:16; 14:1-2).
2. God is merciful (2 Kings 17:1-6).
3. God is slow to anger (2 Kings 17:7-23).
4. God is kind (2 Kings 17:24-41).

The verse to be memorized:

Turn unto the LORD your God: for He is gracious and merciful, slow to anger, and of great kindness. (Joel 2:13b)

THE LESSON

The true and living God of heaven is "holy." That is, He is absolutely *perfect*, set apart from all others. He is *righteous* and always does right. He is *pure*, without any sin.

Long ago, God, the holy One, chose a particular family for Himself. He chose a homeland for them. In time, the family settled in God's land. The father of the family was Jacob, whose name God had changed to Israel (Genesis 32:28). So the homeland of God's people was called Israel. Years later, because of King Solomon's sin, God's wonderful nation was torn apart. The smaller southern part of the nation was called Judah. (This was the name of its larger tribe.) The larger northern part kept the name Israel. (Review Volume 23, Lesson 3.)

Jeroboam was the first king of Israel, the Northern Kingdom. Because King Jeroboam was wicked, he set up idols in the land. "Worship these!" he commanded. So the people turned from God to worship golden calf idols. Therefore Jeroboam became known as "the king who caused Israel to sin." (See, for example, 1 Kings 12:28-32; 2 Kings 13:6, 11; 14:24; 15:9, 18, 24, 28.) What a dreadful reputation! Every Israelite king who followed Jeroboam was sinful also.

1. GOD IS GRACIOUS
Joel 2:13; Hosea 4:1-2; 11:1-8; 13:16; 14:1-2

God loved His people of both parts of the nation–Israel and Judah. So when they sinned, God sent **prophets** to warn them. The **prophet JOEL** spoke the words of our verse to the people of Judah. He said, "Turn unto the Lord, your God; for He is gracious and merciful, slow to anger, and of great kindness" (Joel 2:13).

"God is *gracious*," **JOEL** said. That is, *God shows favor, even to those who do not deserve it*. God is also fair. He who is holy must punish those who sin.

God sent the **prophet HOSEA** to the people of Israel. "Hear the word of the Lord, you Israelites!" **Hosea** announced. "The Lord has a charge against you. You are not faithful nor do you show love. You do not admit that God is your Lord. You swear, lie, kill, steal, and commit adultery." (See Hosea 4:1-2.)

God's people were breaking these five of the Ten Commandments. God had given these commands when He first chose Israel for Himself. (See Exodus 20:1-17.) So His people had always known His laws.

Show Illustration #14

God spoke lovingly to His people through **HOSEA**. " 'When Israel was a child, I loved him . . . I taught the Israelites to walk, taking them by the arms . . . I led them with kindness and love.' " (See **Hosea** 11:1, 3-4.) As a father loves his child, so God loved His people. He gave them commandments so they would know how to live. He loved them, taught them, fed them. Sadly, God had to say: "My people are determined to turn from Me. How can I give you up?" (See Hosea 11:7-8.)

Finally, God said through His **prophet**; "The people have rebelled against their God. They shall fall by the sword; their infants shall be dashed to pieces." (See Hosea 13:16.) Like a loving father, God once more pled: "O Israel, return to the Lord, your God. You have fallen by your sin. Turn to the Lord. Say to Him, 'Take away all sin and receive us graciously.' " (See Hosea 14:1-2.)

2. GOD IS MERCIFUL
2 Kings 17:1-6

A time came when the Israelite people were filled with fear. Assyria (400 miles to the north-east–show on map) had conquered one country after another. Now Assyria's king was slowly moving his army into Israel. Finally the king of Israel became the servant of the king of Assyria.

Israel's king announced to his people: "We need more money for the king of Assyria." So the Israelites paid and paid and paid the Assyrian king. Finally they did not pay. So the Assyrian king decided the Israelite king was a traitor.

Show Illustration #15A

The king of Assyria threw Israel's king into prison. Then the Assyrian army marched against the entire land of Israel. They attacked Samaria, the capital city and fought against it three years. At last the Assyrians captured Samaria and the Israelites. They marched the Israelites to many places in Assyria, far, far from their homeland.

God could have allowed the Israelites to be killed. But He who is holy and gracious, is also merciful. That is, *He is good to those who do not deserve it*. Long, long before, God had told His people: "If you do not obey the Lord your God, the Lord will cause you to be defeated by your enemies. Your dead bodies will be food for the birds of the air and the beasts of the earth." (See Deuteronomy 28:15, 26.) This time God was merciful to Israel. He did not allow all His people to be killed. Instead, He caused them to be taken to Assyria. Years before, God had sent **JONAH** to preach in Assyria's capital city. And the Assyrians had then turned to the Lord. Maybe now the Israelites would turn back to God.

It was dreadful to see God's people taken as prisoners of war. Each one was like a bird with a broken wing, fluttering on the ground.

Show Illustration #15B

But through the **prophet HOSEA**, God said, " 'You belong to Me in a special way. You have My loving-kindness and mercies.' " (See Hosea 2:19.) God's people were in His hands, even though they were prisoners of Assyria. God, the holy One, is merciful.

3. GOD IS SLOW TO ANGER
2 Kings 17:7-23

In God's Word He tells exactly why He had punished the Israelites. (*Teacher:* Depending on the age of your students, read 2 Kings 17:9-12 from the Bible.)

This is what God Himself said, "I punished the Israelites because they worshiped other gods. They followed the practices of the nations which previously lived in the land. The Israelites did wickedly against God. They had idols on every high hill and under every leafy tree. They burned incense to their idols, called them gods, and made Me angry. I warned them against worshiping idols. But they would not listen. They disobeyed My laws."

Show Illustration #16

God tells more about His sinful people. "I had given them My commands (then written on scrolls). And I sent prophets with My messages. But they would not listen. They disobeyed Me. They turned away from My Laws. They made for themselves two idols in the shape of calves. They bowed down to the stars. They worshiped Baal. They sacrificed their sons and daughters in the fire. So I was very angry with Israel." (See 2 Kings 17:13-18.)

God had earlier sent His **prophet**, **HOSEA**, to warn Israel. Speaking for God, **HOSEA** said, "'The Israelites make idols for themselves with their silver and gold. Throw out your calf-idol, O Israel! My anger burns against them. This calf–a man has made it; it is not God.'" (See Hosea 8:4-6.)

For worshiping idols only one day, God could have been very angry. But Israel worshiped their calf idols 10 days . . . 50 days . . . 100 days . . . 10 years . . . 50 years . . . 100 years . . . 150 years . . . 200 years! Exactly as **JOEL** the **prophet** had said in our verse: "God is slow to anger."

Finally God couldn't allow His people to continue sinning. So He sent the Israelites away "from His presence." He let their enemies capture them and march them off as slaves. These enemies, the Assyrians, led the Israelites to Assyria. (Show on map.) God permitted His very own people to be taken to a foreign land. (See 2 Kings 17:22-23.) There they would live among their enemies. God is slow to anger. But because He is holy, He cannot allow sin to go unpunished. He had to punish His people.

So the people of Israel were torn from their wonderful homeland. What a dreadful day for God's own special people!

4. GOD IS KIND
2 Kings 17:24-41

Israel, the land God had chosen for His chosen people, now belonged to Assyria. So the king of Assyria sent many of his people to live in Israel. The Assyrians did not worship the true and living God of heaven. They brought to Israel their own idols and prayed to them. So God sent lions which killed some of the Assyrians.

The remaining Assyrians rushed word to their king: "The people you sent to live in Israel do not know what the God of this land requires. He has sent lions which are killing our people."

The Assyrian king ordered one of his men: "Get a priest who came from Israel. Send him back to Israel. He is to live there and teach the people what the God of that land requires."

Show Illustration #17

So one of God's priests went to live in Bethel. Do you remember what King Jeroboam had placed in Bethel MOre than 200 years before? (*One of the golden calves which the Israelites worshiped*) Now the priest taught the people how to worship the true God. (See 2 Kings 17:28.)

God is loving and kind. He wanted the Assyrians to know Him. In time the Assyrians went through the motions of worshiping God. But they really did not turn to Him. Those who truly love God worship Him alone. The Assyrians *seemed* to worship God, but they also worshiped idols.

God's priest would have taught the Assyrians God's early commands: "You shall have no other gods but Me. You shall not make for yourself any carved image, or any likeness of anything that is in heaven above, or that is in the earth beneath, or that is in the water under the earth. You shall not bow down to them, nor serve them." (See Exodus 20:4-5.) The Assyrians listened. But they did not obey God's commandments. (See 2 Kings 17:34.)

Today, God wants you and me to worship Him alone. Do you have idols that replace your love for God? You do not have to pray to something to worship it. An idol is anything which is more important to you than God. It could be money, or friends, or "wanting to be first." What is most important in your life? If it is not God, then you have an idol.

Will you talk to God right now about your idol? Admit it to Him. Tell Him you know it is wrong. Ask Him to help you get rid of it. He is loving and kind and willing to forgive you. Tell Him you want to worship Him alone. (*Teacher:* Use 1 John 5:21.)

www.ingramcontent.com/pod-product-compliance
Lightning Source LLC
Chambersburg PA
CBHW060802090426
42736CB00002B/128